THE CARE OF MONKEY HANDBOOK

Alkeith O Jackson

Copyright Notice

CONTENTS

Alkeith O Jackson

THE CARE OF MONKEY HANDBOOK

EXPERT ADVICE ON

HOUSING, FEEDING AND HEALTH

Monkeys And Their Relatives

If you visit a menagerie you will always find a crowd around the monkey cage; even the elephants and lions fail to attract the same interest and attention as these lively and familiar little creatures. Monkeys are so droll, so mischievous, and so human in their ways that they are irresistible, and even the hurrying business man will stop to watch the antics of a monkey on the sidewalk.

Many members of the monkey race are exceedingly intelligent and learn to eat at table, dress and undress, go to bed, sweep rooms, ride bicycles, use roller-skates, and even to smoke pipes, like human beings.

These are usually manlike monkeys, or apes, but some of the larger baboons are almost as intelligent. The apes and baboons are not, however, suitable for home pets; they are very valuable and require a great deal of care; they are subject to numerous ills, very susceptible to colds, and the baboons, at least, are usually ill-tempered and often savage, especially toward strangers.

Many of the smaller monkeys make excellent pets, however; but all monkeys require far more care and attention than other pets, and you cannot expect to keep a monkey as easily as you would a cat, dog, or rabbit. There is a vast number of species in the monkey tribe, and they range in size from the giant gorillas, chimpanzees, and orangs, which are nearly as large as a man, to the tiny "Titis," or Squirrel-Monkeys, which are less than a foot in length.

Monkeys are native in both the Old and the New World, but those in America may be readily distinguished from all other species by their noses. Whereas all Old World monkeys have the nostrils pointed or directed downward and close together, the American monkeys all have the nostrils widely separated and directed outward.

The tail of a monkey is often a very good means of determining his nationality; for while the Old World monkeys and the American monkeys may have long tails, short tails, or scarcely any tail at all, the prehensile or grasping form of tail is found only among American monkeys.

If you see a monkey with a prehensile tail you can be sure he is an American; but a short tail or a tail which is not prehensile does not prove that the owner is a foreigner. Most American monkeys are fairly small, the largest being the howlers which are 3 or 4 feet in length, and a member of nearly any species is easily tamed and becomes very affectionate.

The Old World monkeys, on the other hand, vary greatly in size, and many of the species are savage, sullen, and untamable. Practically all hand-organ monkeys are American, and the vast majority of small monkeys in menageries and zoological gardens are also natives of this hemisphere. They are cheaper, hardier, and, as a rule, far more intelligent than the Old World species, and their hand-like tails make them far more interesting and amusing.

Although there are many species of American monkeys, they may be divided into six groups or classes, aside from the marmosets.

The first of these groups comprises the various howlers, big, ill-tempered creatures which troop through the forest tree tops in great droves and make night hideous with their terrific cries. They are practically untamable, and even when treated with the utmost kindness they remain sullen and ferocious.

The Uakaris Monkey

Baboon Monkeys

The second group comprises the queer uakaris. These are baboon-like monkeys, with long, white hair, very short tails, and scarlet faces. They are very rare in captivity and do not thrive outside of their native forests. The couxios, or Bearded Monkeys, are the third group, and these are distinguished by the odd wig-like mop of hair on the crown and by a heavy beard on the chin.

They are strikingly peculiar creatures and look like tiny gnomes or dwarfs. Their tails are not prehensile but are thick and bushy, and the fur is usually long and coarse, although some species have very soft, silky hair.

They vary in color according to the species, but the majority is dark or even black. They are quite small, about 10 or 12 inches in length without the tail, and are easily tamed and become very strongly attached to their masters. They are quite rare in collections but have lots of excellent traits and are so droll in appearance that they deserve to be better known.

The next group contains the so-called Spider- Monkeys. These are the most abundant of American monkeys and are exceedingly active, lively creatures, perfectly at home in the tree tops but are very awkward on the ground on account of their extremely long, slender limbs. Their tails are as useful as a fifth hand and are often used for picking fruit or for carrying food to the mouth; and, as the hands have no thumbs, such a tail is almost a necessity.

Some species of Spider Monkeys are very large; they sometimes reach a length of over 2 feet without the long tail, but they are so lean and "spidery" that they look far longer than they really are.

There are many species of Spider-Monkeys, and they are widely hunted by the natives for food. Their flesh is very sweet and tender and tastes like quail or pigeon. Some Spider-Monkeys are black, others brown, and others a rich reddish color.

Their heads are small, and their expression rather wistful and surprised. They are far from beautiful, but their dispositions are so mild and they are so easily tamed that they are great favorites as pets.

Many Spider-Monkeys show remarkable intelligence; they are easily made unhappy by cross or impatient language and are pleased and encouraged by kind words. They are not nearly as mischievous as many other species and are seldom surly, ill-tempered, or treacherous. They can be trained to perform many odd tricks.

A lady friend who owned a large red Spider-Monkey in Central America had taught the creature to open and shut windows and doors, carry dishes to and from the table, and perform various other household duties. In accomplishing these tasks the monkey never ran on all fours but hopped along on its hind limbs, using its tail as a prop or support, or at times carrying some object in its grasp.

The Capuchins Monkey

The capuchins are another group or class of American monkeys which includes numerous varieties. They are easily recognized by an extremely long prehensile tail, thickly covered with hair, a well-developed thumb on the hand, and a large, intelligent head covered with short hair.

These are the commonest of all American monkeys in menageries, and nearly all hand-organ monkeys belong in this group. In color they are variable; some varieties are brown, others gray, others golden, others reddish, and some very dark-brown or even black.

In nearly all varieties the head and face are lighter in color than the rest of the body, and in the White-Faced Monkeys the whole face, throat, neck, and chest are pure white.

The capuchins are exceedingly intelligent but restless, inquisitive, and changeable in mood. They are usually good-tempered and although seldom malicious are very mischievous and full of tricks.

The capuchins make very affectionate and interesting pets but are often extremely jealous and fly into a perfect fury of rage if their master or mistress shows any attention to other creatures or to human beings. They are also very uncomfortable when laughed at and will often sulk for hours and utter most pitiful cries if scolded or punished. These monkeys often form sudden attachments to strangers and whine and cry if their affection is not returned.

They are tireless investigators and will spend a great deal of time endeavoring to solve the mystery of a watch or other mechanical device and are as pleased as children when they discover how to use some tool or a utensil such as a comb, brush, mirror, or cup. They are quite hardy and withstand changes in climate and temperature far better than most monkeys.

The last group of American monkeys comprises the Titis, or Squirrel-Monkeys. These are very small, gentle creatures with long hairy tails which are not at all prehensile. The colors are usually bright reddish, or golden-brown, and the fur is soft, thick, and silky.

The face is often white or very pale-colored, and the eyes are large, soft, and gentle. The Squirrel-Monkeys are very easily tamed and love to be petted and caressed. They like warmth and shelter and will sleep contentedly in their owner's pocket or curled in one's lap. They are by far the most desirable of the true monkeys for house pets and are as cleanly and neat as squirrels.

The Marmosets Monkey

These are the most beautiful and lovable of all the monkey family. In size they are about as large as a squirrel, and they are so gentle and affectionate that they are always great favorites. There are several species—all American—and in habits, appearance, and other characteristics they are all much alike. Marmosets require a great deal of warmth and should always be kept in a warm room with plenty of soft bedding.

In cold weather, a warm soapstone wrapped in several thicknesses of flannel will make a nice cozy bed for the little creatures, but ordinarily a nest of soft wool and cotton will keep them warm enough. They soon learn to creep into a tiny bed and will snuggle down under the miniature blankets in a very human-like manner.

They are very easily tamed and may be allowed the liberty of a room without the least danger, for they seldom attempt to hide or escape but prefer to cuddle up in one's lap or curl up inside of a pocket or a basket of cloth. They are apt to be very timid in the presence of strangers and keep up a querulous little cry if they are alarmed or distrustful.

In summer-time marmosets may be kept out-of doors during the day, and I have known of several cases where tame marmosets were allowed to roam at large about the garden. These little creatures made no effort to escape but travelled here and there along the fences and among shrubbery, or dozed in the sun.

They kept well out of the reach of dogs, which they seemed to recognize as natural enemies. At first the owner of these marmosets was afraid they would be caught or injured by stray cats, but the cats seemed to consider the marmosets as uncanny and gave them a wide berth.

Marmosets may be kept in small cages with perches and swings, or they may be secured with a light chain or cord attached to a collar or belt and fastened to a shelf or box provided with a nest. They should be kept very neat and clean, and their coats should be daily brushed with a child's soft hair-brush.

Fresh water should always be within reach, and in cold weather it should be about the temperature of the room. If you see a marmoset shivering or wrapped up in its tail you may be sure that it feels chilly, and it should immediately be moved to a warmer spot.

In their wild state marmosets live upon small birds, bird eggs, insects, and fruit. In captivity they should be fed on fruit, mocking-bird food, canary and other seeds, meal worms, and insects, with now and then a little finely minced raw chicken or meat.

Sometimes marmosets are very fond of milk, and a reasonable amount will not hurt them. Hard-boiled egg is also excellent, especially in cold weather, and if you can secure some eggs of the English sparrows they will prove a most enjoyable tidbit for your pets.

Old World Monkeys

Aside from the baboons, mandrills, macaques, and the large apes, none of which are suitable for home pets, the Old World monkeys are comparatively few in number and many of the most beautiful and interesting species are very rare or are seldom found in captivity.

The commonest of the foreign monkeys in captivity is the Green Monkey, so called from the color of its fur, which is an olive-green. The face is decorated with long whitish, or yellow whiskers, which unite over the forehead, and the throat and under-parts are also whitish.

The Green Monkey is a native of Africa but was introduced into the West Indies about the year 1700, and is now very abundant on the islands of Saint Kitts and Grenada.

Green Monkeys

The Mangabeys

The mangabeys are somewhat like the Green Monkeys in form but are very different in color. They are usually dark or blackish with small whiskers, projecting eyebrows, and white eyelids. Some species have white heads and light lower parts; others have a white collar, while still others are entirely black.

Related to these is the Diana Monkey, a species with a grizzly-black coat, with the forehead, a goat-like beard, the throat, chest, inside of legs, and a streak across the rump, pure white. It is a beautiful species and easily tamed.

The Bonnet

The Bonnet-Monkey is a peculiar species from India, where it is held sacred by the natives, and being unmolested, it commits great depredations on growing crops. The color is yellowish, with black hands and feet, and the hair on the head projects over the eyes and around the cheeks in such a way that the animal seems to be wearing a bonnet.

These monkeys are easily tamed and become quite affectionate, but when fully grown are too large to make good pets. An adult Bonnet-Monkey will weigh twenty-five pounds or more and is a very large and strong creature.

The Orange-Faced Monkey

The Orange-Faced Monkey of China is a very beautiful creature with its golden face surrounded by glossy white whiskers, and a line of reddish-brown across the eyebrows. The back is dove-gray with a square patch of white on the loins.

The tail and arms are white, and a collar of bright chestnut surrounds the lower neck. The thighs are black and the hind legs brownish red. It is rarely seen in this country but makes an excellent pet.

The Guereza Monkey

Possibly the most beautiful of all monkeys is the African guereza. This animal has the limbs, back, and head covered with short, glossy, jet-black fur with the cheeks, chin, and forehead pure white. Hanging from the sides, flanks, and end of the tail is a long, luxurious fringe of silky white hair which gives the monkey a most elegant appearance.

The guereza is much hunted for its skin, is rather rare in collections, and is seldom seen in captivity, although it is easily tamed and makes a very handsome and interesting pet. Many other species of both American and foreign monkeys are seen in menageries and for sale by dealers, but the varieties described above are the more desirable of those commonly offered for sale.

In selecting a monkey for a pet, be sure that it is healthy and good-tempered. Many monkeys are cross and savage in the presence of strangers, and you should not judge hastily of the animal's nature by a single visit to the dealer's.

If you like monkeys try to make friends with it, feed it a few dainties, and coax it, talking quietly to it meanwhile, and in this way overcoming its shyness and distrust. After a few visits it will probably recognize you, and if it appears to take a liking to you and allows you to stroke or scratch it you may be confident that it will make a good pet.

Diseases

Chelada Monkey

Monkeys have numerous diseases, but as most of them are very similar to human ills they may be successfully treated by the same remedies that you would employ for like ailments in a child. Colds, influenza, and pneumonia are their commonest troubles, and these ills are easier to prevent than to cure. Improper food and overfeeding are also the cause of many monkey diseases. It is an all too common habit to feed monkeys everything and anything that they like.

Lemurs

You may think that monkeys are interesting and amusing pets, and that the dainty marmosets are very lovable, but if you once keep a pet lemur you will find that it combines all the desirable qualities and characters of both monkeys and marmosets, with none of the bad traits of the former and far more intelligence than the latter.

Lemurs, although related to monkeys, are very different from those animals in appearance. The sharp nose and foxlike face, with its staring owl-like eyes give the lemurs a very wide-awake and knowing expression, and they have a cool, odd manner of peering fixedly at any object which is very amusing.

The perfectly formed fingers and thumbs resemble the lean, wrinkled hands of an old dark-skin person, while the long, bushy, and beautiful tail is far handsomer than that of any squirrel. There are many species of lemurs, but the majority is natives of Madagascar and East Africa, and all are more or less similar and are easily recognized.

Lemurs are naturally nocturnal, but in confinement they soon learn to stay awake during the day, and they prove one of the most interesting, affectionate, and intelligent of all pet animals. They are wonderfully active creatures, with the power of making prodigious leaps or bounds, and will jump from and alight upon narrow or insecure footholds with the ease and agility of a bird.

Their hands are not only fitted for grasping by the form of the fingers and thumbs, but in addition many species possess the power of actually causing the palms of their feet to adhere to a perfectly smooth surface by means of tiny, sucker-like wrinkles and papillae.

The lemurs readily walk erect, and in cages they have a curious habit of running back and forth on a perch while standing on the hind feet, and keeping the front feet clasped over the breast. Although usually quite silent, the lemurs possess voices out of all proportion to their size, and the cry of a small lemur sounds more like the roar of a lion than the call of such a dainty little creature.

The lemur's tail is its pride and delight. A tame lemur will squat for hours fondling and arranging its tail, and when cold the little creature uses it for a blanket and swings it over one shoulder in a very jaunty manner, reminding one of a Mexican with his serape. When sleeping the lemur curls up in a ball and wraps itself in its bushy tail, and then appears like a mere ball of soft fur.

Lemurs grow very fond of their masters and trot around after them most assiduously, often clinging with one hand to the edge of a garment and holding the voluminous tail over the other arm. They soon learn to run up and down stairs, and seem to delight in imitating the actions and attitudes of human beings. They are very inquisitive but are never mischievous or malicious like monkeys.

They love to investigate a strange person or a new object, but seem to feel that everyone is a friend, and are willing, to be petted or stroked by any one, and are greatly pleased at any attention shown them.

They are extremely docile, and I never knew of a lemur biting or snapping at any one; in fact, their teeth rather preclude the idea of their biting seriously, for they are adapted to eating fruits and soft-bodied insects rather than to tearing meat or breaking hard-shelled nuts.

Lemurs are natives of tropical countries and must be kept warm and free from draughts, but they are such delightful pets and so cleanly in their habits and free from any disagreeable odor that no one will find it too much trouble to give them all the care and attention they require.

Lemurs may be kept in good-sized squirrel cages or in houses made of wire netting, and when they become accustomed to their new home and are thoroughly acquainted with their owners they may be released from their cage a great deal of the time. During warm summer weather they may be taken out-of-doors, and they will romp and play in great glee, and will find a lot of exercise and delight in scratching about for insects.

The body of the commoner species of lemurs is about 15 to 16 inches in length, with a tail measuring as much more, but they are very light in weight and the thick fur makes them look much larger than they really are.

In a wild state the lemur feeds upon fruits and insects exclusively, and in confinement it should be fed upon dates, bananas, insects, and sweetened and softened rice and grain. Meal-worms, ants' eggs, and insects should also be fed freely and water should be given. Some lemurs are fond of fresh vegetables and grass, and others seem to require a little meat now and then. The best diet is a varied one, as for monkeys and marmosets, but fruit should be the main article of food.

Cleanliness is as essential for lemurs as for any other pet, and as they are naturally very clean and neat animals any dirt or a foul cage is very distasteful to them; in fact, I have known of a lemur absolutely to refuse to eat or sleep in a cage which had not been properly cleaned.

They are not at all difficult to keep, and are seldom troubled with any disease other than colds or influenza, which may be prevented by keeping them warm and protected from draughts.

On cold nights they should be placed in a warm spot, and the cage may be wrapped in cloth or paper as an additional protection. Lemurs seldom have fleas or other vermin, and as far as I know there is absolutely no objectionable feature about them. If you want a really interesting, odd, and beautiful pet by all means obtain a lemur.

Feeding Your Monkey

In a wild state monkeys live on a very mixed and miscellaneous diet of nuts, fruits, seeds, shoots, leaves, birds, insects, eggs, and vegetables. Some species feed largely upon animal matter, and others subsist almost wholly upon vegetable food, but in confinement a mixed diet is always preferable. The principal food should consist of grains, fruit, and fresh green vegetables.

Nuts may be given sparingly as luxuries, but roasted peanuts should never be given. I doubt if any food is worse for a monkey than roasted peanuts, although monkeys in menageries are constantly receiving them. Cooked food of any sort is unnatural, and peanuts are very indigestible. Probably more digestive disorders among caged monkeys can be traced to peanuts than to anything else.

The mainstay of a monkey's diet should be grain and vegetables. Cracked corn, paddy, hemp, rape, and canary-seed, as well as oats and wheat, should be fed freely. Any fresh vegetables, especially raw sweet potatoes, carrots, artichokes, beets, and the like are all excellent.

Ripe apples, bananas, oranges, and other fruits are also good, and some species of monkeys will subsist almost entirely upon fruit. Meal-worms and ants' eggs should be given every day or two, and any other insects, either fresh or prepared as directed for soft-billed birds, should be given whenever possible.

Raw chicken eggs are relished, and you will be surprised to see how neatly a monkey will open and eat a chicken's egg without spilling any of the contents. Fresh green clover and lettuce should be offered to the monkey, for some individuals are very fond of greens.

If your monkey will drink milk it will not harm it, but it should be given with a little lime-water, and preferably scalded. Sugar, candy, cake, pie, and all other sweet substances should be avoided.

All such foods are injurious, but a piece of sugar-cane or

a green cornstalk will be a welcome and healthy addition to the monkey's bill of fare. In summer the animal may be given raw green corn on the cob, as well as raw peas, beans, and other vegetables. Corn should never be given in large quantities in any form as it is heating, but in winter it may be given more liberally than in summer.

Dry, hard bread crusts will seldom prove injurious, but soft or newly baked bread should never be fed. Many monkeys must have a limited amount of animal food. If the monkey seems to be dissatisfied with its diet, try a little raw chicken or beef and if it appears to relish it feed it a very little once or twice a week.

Be very careful not to overfeed. Monkeys are greedy creatures and will eat all they can hold and then stuff their cheek-pouches full. Just as soon as you see the monkey begin to fill its cheeks with food stop feeding, and give a little less the next time.

Feed three times a day, morning, noon, and night, and try to plan the meals so that each contains different substances. If the monkey appears hungry between meals and cries out when you approach, you can increase the amount of food slightly until it appears satisfied.

A dish of hard, whole grains may be left within reach all the time, for monkeys will seldom eat more than they require of these things and the mastication required is good for them.

As each species of monkey varies more or less in its likes and dislikes respecting food, and every individual of a species have personal preferences just as people do, it is impossible to lay down a hard-and-fast rule for all monkeys. Use common sense, judgment, and a varied diet, and you will soon learn your monkey's tastes and what it is best to feed it.

Care And Housing

Monkeys are all natives of warm countries and are very susceptible to changes of climate and cold weather. Draughts, dampness, and unusual cold are fatal to them, and probably more monkeys die from pneumonia and pleurisy than from any other causes. Keep your monkeys in a well-heated, properly ventilated room in cold weather and do not expose them to draughts or sudden changes of air.

Never open a window when a monkey is in the room in cold weather, and never keep a monkey's cage on the floor where it is draughty. Most monkeys love the warmth and brightness of sunshine, and a sun-bath is good for them. Extreme cleanness of food, cage, and the animal itself is a prime factor in maintaining monkeys in good health, and the cage should be thoroughly cleaned and disinfected each day.

Do not keep a monkey cooped up in a small cage. They are very lively, active animals by nature and must have abundant opportunity for exercise if they are to thrive in captivity. Even a small monkey should have a cage at least 3 feet square and 3 or 4 feet in height, and if you cannot provide such quarters you should not think of keeping a monkey. The little Titis and marmosets may, however, be kept in a good sized squirrel cage, especially if allowed to exercise in the room or yard each day.

It is not necessary to have a ready-made wire cage; an ordinary wire-netting cage is just as good or better, and in such a cage you may have a scraggly tree or some branches which the inmate will thoroughly appreciate.

The cage should be provided with a snug box or nest, for monkeys love comfort and warmth when sleeping, but the nest materials should be renewed every few days and the box thoroughly disinfected.

Cover the floor of the cage with clean, fine sawdust, sprinkled with eucalyptus-oil and water, and renew it each day, and give the animal some bright-colored, large-sized marbles, a toy china doll, or some other toys to play with. Monkeys will amuse themselves with toys by the hour, and are as fond of such things as children.

Always provide clean drinking water in abundance, and if you secure your pet by a belt and chain be very sure that the belt is not too tight. Monkeys brought to this country by seamen are often fastened with a chain to a belt, and frequently the belt is so tight that it seriously injures the monkey.

It is a wise plan always to examine a new monkey to be sure that an old belt or cord does not still encircle the animal's waist. Sometimes the belt may be left in place and so concealed by the hair that it is not noticeable. I have known of cases in which a sick and apparently dying monkey was completely cured in a few days by removing a piece of leather thong which was tied about the creature's waist and was concealed by its fur.

Many people object to tame monkeys on the ground that they carry fleas, lice, bedbugs, and other vermin. It must be admitted that far too many monkeys are afflicted with these detestable pests, but they are easily destroyed and will not return if the monkey is kept clean, and other monkeys, dogs, or cats with fleas are not allowed near.

When you first acquire a monkey treat its fur with a good dose of fresh Persian Insect-Powder, rubbing the powder well into the roots of the hair. It will doubtless object to the process, but if necessary it may be muzzled during it.

Repeat the operation again in two days, and in the meantime keep the cage well sprayed with disinfectant. After the second application remove the monkey from the cage and scald the entire cage with boiling water.

Brush out the monkey's fur thoroughly, and you will have no further trouble with vermin if you have carried out the treatment properly. If there are fleas or other vermin on the head near the eyes and nostrils, do not use the powder in these places, but rub Vaseline and sulphur well into the roots of the hair.

Alkeith O Jackson

Baboon Monkey

Barbary Ape Monkey

Barbary Ape Monkey

Proboscis Monkey

Alkeith O Jackson

Proboscis Monkey

Orangutan

Alkeith O Jackson

Printed in Great Britain
by Amazon

35302516R00027